THE DAVIES CAEADDA FAMILY

By Antony David Davies

I0448047

Cover photo Caeadda thanks to Dafydd Pughe

© 2014 by Antony David Davies. All rights reserved.

No part of this book may be reproduced in any written, electronic, recording, or photocopying form without written permission of the author, Antony David Davies.

I would like to dedicate this book to all of my ancestors who lived and farmed so successfully at Caeadda for so many years. Their hard work and success in life has allowed me to research and write this fascinating book based on their lives. But in particular I would like to dedicate this book to the memory of my grandfather Griffith Llewelyn Davies. Without the curiosity to know about him this book would never have been written.

Griffith Llewelyn Davies

Contents

Introduction

As a young child growing up away from my ancestral home of Llanwrin I had no knowledge of my ancestors. Indeed, I actually had no knowledge whatsoever about my grandfather. I had only a vague idea that his name was "Griff." I never heard him mentioned and never saw a photo of him until I was twenty. After leaving school I briefly worked in the Powys County Archives, and having a free afternoon I decided to see if I could find anything out about "Griff Davies." It was at this moment that I discovered the Davies Caeadda family.

This happened in the late 1990s. Since that date on and off I have dedicated myself to finding out about who my ancestors were and what they did in life. It is with a sense of pride that I can now boast that my family has farmed the same land now for nearly three hundred years.

This book offers a glimpse into what I have discovered. It goes back to the very establishment of the Davies surname and continues the history of the family right up until the death of my cousin Trevor Owen Davies in 1966. Therefore this can be said to be a family history from 1700 until 1966. I end this book with 1966 as that date marks the end of the Davies surname itself being associated with Caeadda, as thereafter the farm passed down a female line of the Davies family. So hopefully this manuscript will provide a good account of the Davies years. I would urge the reader to consult the contents page, as this should distinguish the different generations.

As an accompaniment to this book there is a website, www.daviescaeadda.co.uk which also chronicles the family history and where the author can be contacted. This is a first edition work, and I welcome any further information regarding the family and would make future editions available to include any future information.

In writing this book I have consulted a number of sources. Namely the Library of Wales Newspaper Archive, the books *From Wales to Wood River, Immigration and Settlement 1870-1939, Shepherds and Shepherding*, and various parish registers, namely the ones covering Llanwrin.

Finally I would like to thank my uncle, Glyn Davies, and cousins Dafydd Pughe and Carys Jones for all their help and invaluable information.

Antony David Davies

Early Cilgwyn Family

The earliest ancestor so far discovered is a man named David Thomas, or Dafydd ap Tomos – or in plain English David the son of Thomas. At this time the Welsh did not use surnames as are now common in modern day Wales. For centuries the Welsh used the patronymic naming system. In this system the names changed with each generation. Therefore using or David Thomas as an example we know he was the son of a man called Thomas. The patronymic system also applied to women. For example, if Thomas had a daughter she would have been known as Mary verch Tomos.

David Thomas was born in about 1713, but unfortunately his birth place is currently a mystery. What is certain is that he was not from Llanwrin, as nobody matching him was baptised in the parish church between 1700 and 1730. However, we can probably be fairly sure he was from the surrounding area of north Montgomeryshire or south Merionethshire. The first near certain mention of David Thomas occurs on the 26th January 1734 when he married Elinor John in the parish church in Llanwrin. Elinor appears to have been a daughter of John ap Dafydd ap Rhydderch (who died in 1744). Elinor's family certainly did come from Llanwrin. Her family had been farming in the area at least since the 1500s. Interestingly a man named Hugh Rhydderch was farming as Esgair Llewelyn when he died in 1701 – we shall hear more about this particular farm later.

David and Elinor appear to have started farming at Cilgwyn, presumably shortly after their marriage in 1734. So far I have discovered that they had at least six children – Mary, Thomas, David, Susan, Elinor and Hugh. All of these children appear to have started using the surname of David/Davies. Common surnames had started to be adopted by the Welsh during the reign of Henry VIII in the 1500s, and in time spread around the country. Initially to have a standard surname in Wales was a symbol of wealth and status. So we can say with near certainty that the Davies surname started in the 1730s, or at least the mid eighteenth century. Therefore all of us remaining Davies's of the family can say we are named after David Thomas of Cilgwyn.

David Thomas died at Cilgwyn aged about seventy two on the 7th January 1785. He was buried in the church cemetery in Llanwrin on the 11th January. His wife Elinor died aged about ninety at Cilgwyn and was buried in Llanwrin on the 8th May 1802.

Hugh Davies succeeded his father at Cilgwyn in 1785. On the 20th October 1782 he married Jane Pugh in Llanwrin. She was one of the daughters of Lewis Pugh who farmed at Aberffrydlan in Llanwrin. The couple had at least ten children. Hugh remained farming at Cilgwyn until at least 1807. When he died aged seventy four in 1826 he was described as of "Glandovey." There is no evidence that any of his sons farmed at Cilgwyn, therefore we can perhaps assume that the family left the farm sometime between 1807 and 1826. Hugh's eldest son David Davies (1783-1848) married Elinor Davies of the Davies Esgair Hir family (who we will learn more about later). The fate of the children of Hugh and Jane currently remain a mystery, as all of them appear to have left the Llanwrin area. However, I have discovered the sad story of his daughter Susan Davies (1799-1881). In 1831 she married Evan Vaughan (1791-1858) in Llanwrin. By 1841 the couple were claiming poor relief off the parish. After Evan's death Susan ended up in the Machynlleth Workhouse. On the 1871 census she was described as being "weak minded" and in 1881 as being an "imbecile."

The First Davies Caeadda Family

Caeadda has now been linked to the Davies family for over two hundred years. The earliest mention that I have found regarding Caeadda is a will from 1717 for a woman named Eleanor Herbert who lived at "Cae Adda Goch." In 1744 a woman named Catherine John died at "Cae Adda Felin." In 1760 a man named Hugh Thomas died at Caeadda. He was buried in Llanwrin of the 14th July 1760. He had been living there for some time, as his son Thomas was born on the farm in 1727. Whether Hugh Thomas and David Thomas were related is unknown, but at present we cannot rule out the possibility that they were.

The eldest son of David Thomas and his wife Elinor was Thomas David or Tomos ap Dafydd. He was baptised at the parish church in Llanwrin on the 15th April 1738. He married Mary David (1743-1824) in Llanwrin on the 19th November 1762. At present little is known about Mary and her background, but it is likely that she was a local girl and probably from a farming background. Thomas and Mary had at least seven children. David, Mary, John, Jane, Susanna and Thomas. We shall shortly take a closer look at the more notable children.

One of the children, Jane Davies, was baptised in Llanwrin on the 9th January 1780, and her father was described as being of "Cae Adda." This is the first recorded mention of the family being at Caeadda that has so far discovered. However, I believe it is possible that Thomas Davies moved to Caeadda in 1762/1763 shortly after his marriage. Thomas died aged eighty eight at Caeadda on the 28th September 1826, and his wife Mary had died there at the age of eighty one in January 1824. Both were buried in the churchyard at Llanwrin.

Linking the First Two Generations

So how can we link David Thomas Cilgwyn to our Thomas Davies Caeadda? We are extremely lucky that the grave of David Thomas still exists in the graveyard at Llanwrin church. However, our luck becomes almost unbelievable when we find that David Thomas is buried with his son Thomas Davies. This perfectly links the two generations together. Added to this the Llanwrin parish registers also confirm the information. However, it should be noted that the parish registers do not conclusively prove relationships. For example an entry might read "Thomas son of Thomas and Mary Davies." This very basic form of information makes research much harder when you consider how common the names were in the Llanwrin area at that time. As we enter the early 1800s research gets slightly easier as the registers started recording the farm names in baptisms, marriages and deaths.

Mary Davies – Hendreboeth Family

The eldest daughter of Thomas David and Mary David of Caeadda was Mary Davies. She was baptised in Llanwrin on the 12th May 1768. Presumably Mary was also born at Caeadda. She married David Pugh on the 4th May 1793 in Llanwrin. Initially they loved at Esgair For, but from around 1800 they farmed at Hendreboeth. David died aged sixty four and was buried in Llanwrin on the 10th January 1835. Mary died aged sixty five and was buried in Llanwrin on the 1st June 1833.

They were succeeded at Hendreboeth by their youngest daughter Mary Pugh and her husband John Davies (not related to the main Davies family of this book). Mary was born at Hendreboeth on the 28th March 1808 and baptised in Llanwrin on the 3rd April. On the 22nd June 1833 she married John Davies (1805-1886) in Llanwrin. Mary died aged 77 and was buried in Llanwrin on the 25th May 1885. John died aged eighty one and was buried in Llanwrin on the 15th June 1886. In turn, Mary and John were succeeded by their son David Davies.

David Davies was baptised in Llanwrin on the 16th November 1835. As a young man he worked as a labourer around the farms in the local area. In 1851 he was living and working at Glynceirig, in 1861 he was working as a carter at the rectory for the Reverend Isaac Bonsall, and in 1871 working as a labourer at Dolydd Bychain, Llanwrin. On the 1881 census he was still working as a labourer at Dolydd Bychain. By 1891 he had succeeded his parents at Hendreboeth. In April 1904 David retired from farming and auctioned off the livestock, farming tools and furniture at Hendreboeth. Therefore the family's one hundred year association with the farm came to an end. David then moved to Tymawr, Ceinws, to live with his sister. He died at Tymawr aged sixty nine on the 27th July 1905 of pneumonia. He was buried in Llanwrin. He never married and had no children.

Although the Hendreboeth remained on the same farm for just over one hundred years there is no evidence of prosperity. Indeed they did not reach anywhere near the heights of their Caeadda cousins, and no mention can be found of them in the newspapers of the day.

John Davies was baptised in Llanwrin on the 15th March 1778. In around 1810 he married a girl named Mary from Dolgellau and moved across the border to Shrewsbury. In Shrewsbury he established his own maltser and brewing business. His business premises were somewhere in Chester Street, while John and his family lived in Castle Gates. By the time of his death in 1856, he had achieved a significant level of success. He was succeeded in business by his son John Davies the Younger. John and Mary had at least five children:

Margaret Davies (1814-1888) – she married Edward Lloyd (1817-1894) and relocated to London in the 1850s. The family went into banking, with her son Griffith Evan Lloyd eventually becoming a bank manager in the late 1800s.

Ann Davies (1817-1889) – she married Charles Barron Nicholls (1817-1891) and they lived life as gentry in Shrewsbury living in an elegant residence overlooking the Quarry Park in Shrewsbury. Her husband was the son of Charles Nicholls, a wealthy flannel merchant of Shrewsbury and Welshpool.

Charlotte Davies (1821-1873) – she never married and was a housekeeper to her brother John Davies the Younger.

John Davies the Younger (1823-1888) - by 1871 he had retired and presumably sold the brewing business, and from this time until his death in 1888 he lived the life of a gentleman and owned an elegant residence called Preston House in Shrewsbury. He never married and had no children.

Mary Ann Davies (b.1825) – she married a Shrewsbury draper named Thomas Butler in 1852. Their fates are currently a mystery.

Jane Davies

Jane's baptism gives us our first undisputable mention of Caeadda in connection with the Davies family. On the 15th May 1805 she married Hugh Edwards (1778-1844). In 1841 Jane and Hugh were living at Ogof Fawr in Isygarreg, where Hugh was working as an agricultural labourer. In 1848 Jane was present at Caeadda when her sister-in-law Anne died, as it was Jane who registered the death. The death certificate of Anne Davies also shows us that Jane was not literate as she marked her signature with a cross. Jane appeared once again at Caeadda on the 1851 census. In 1861 she was living with her eldest son, Edward Edwards (born in 1806), and his family in Cynfal Fawr, Merionethshire. At the time Jane was in receipt of poor relief from the parish. She died aged eighty four of old age at Esgair Ucha on the 1st March 1864. Jane and her husband were both buried in Llanwrin.

The Second Thomas Davies Caeadda

The youngest son of first Thomas Davies Caeadda was also called Thomas Davies. He was born at Caeadda on the 22nd February 1788 and was baptised in Llanwrin on the 24th February. He married Anne Davies (1785-1848) on the 3rd February 1826 in Llanwrin. Anne was a daughter of John and Mary Davies who were farming at Esgair Hir in Llanwrin. Anne's mother left a will when she died in 1826, and left "my daughter Anne Davies of Caeadda" two shillings and six pence. Anne's brother, David Davies (1771-1843) farmed at Gwernstablau, Llanwrin. It is interesting to note that Anne's grandson, Thomas Davies (1864-1930) would later farm there as well.

In September 1837 Caeadda was part of an estate that had belonged to the "widowed Ann Jones." Her estate was broken up and sold - the sale took place at the Eagles Hotel in Machynlleth. Thomas Davies was listed as being the tenant farmer and Caeadda was described as being a 144 acre farm.

Anne Davies died at Caeadda aged sixty three of jaundice on the 29 September 1848. She was buried in Llanwrin on the 3rd October 1848. It is likely that Anne was suffering from cancer, which in the 1840s would have been recorded as jaundice. The illness turns the victim's skin and eyes yellow. So Anne likely suffered from liver cancer or a cancer that spread to her liver, such as cancers of the breast, bowels, pancreas, lungs and prostate).

Thomas retired from farming at some point between 1861 and 1871, when his son Thomas took over the running of the farm. Thomas died at Caeadda aged eighty six of bronchitis on the 10th February 1875, and was buried in Llanwrin on the 13th February.

In the early 1800s there was another Davies family farming at Esgair Hir. This was the family of the Anne Davies who married the second Thomas Davies Caeadda. The head of this family was a man named John Davies. So far I have not discovered any information about him. He was married to a woman named Mary. Again, her origins and background are for the moment a mystery. It is, however, possible that John and Mary married in Llanwrin on the 21st December 1765. But for the moment it is uncertain as to where the couple might have come from. All we know for fact is that their children appear to have all been born in Llanwrin. The couple certainly did not farm at Esgair Hir until after 1801, when the farmer Evan Morgan died at the property. Indeed, it might just be possible that John Davies never actually farmed here, it might be that his son Hugh Davies was the only member of this family who ran the farm.

So far I have been unable to find any definite record for John Davies. However, Mary died at Esgair Hir and was buried in Llanwrin on the 9th June 1826. Fortunately she left a will which has been invaluable to building a picture of the Davies Esgair Hir family. The will had been written on the 18th May 1826. So we might be able to assume that the will was written as she was dying.

The eldest child of John and Mary appears to have been John Davies, who was baptised in Llanwrin on the 20th November 1766. According to the 1826 will of Mary Davies he was living in Machynlleth. So far his life and fate is a mystery.

The eldest daughter was Mary Davies who was baptised in Llanwrin on the 21st March 1769. She never married and appears to have spent the majority of her life at Esgair Hir, most likely carrying out the role and duties of a housekeeper. She appears on the 1841 census at Esgair Hir living with her bachelor brother Hugh. After Hugh's death in 1846 she left the farm and went to live with her sister Elinor at Esgair For. Mary died at Esgair For aged eighty two of "old age" on the 12th April 1852. She was buried in Llanwrin on the 15th April 1852.

David Davies was baptised in Llanwrin on the 24th September 1771. He married Jane Williams (1781-1848) in Llanwrin on the 31st May 1805. Jane had inherited the farm of Gwernstablau from her father, Evan Williams, in 1804. David would have taken over the running of the farm after the marriage. David and Jane had a daughter named Anne in 1813, but sadly she died aged only about three months. Another daughter was born at Gwernstablau and also named Anne Davies on the 21st February 1822. She was baptised at the Sion Methodist Chapel in Llanwrin on the 5th March 1822. David died at Gwernstablau aged seventy of "gravel" (kidney stones) on the 17th December 1843. He was buried in Llanwrin on the 19th December 1843. When he died his personal estate was valued at around £400. Sadly his daughter Anne died at Gwernstablau aged only twenty five of consumption (tuberculosis) on the 15th May 1847 and was buried in Llanwrin on the 19th May. With her death the family of David Davies Gwernstablau became extinct. David's widow Jane died at Gwernstablau aged sixty six of consumption (tuberculosis) on the 15th August 1848 and was buried on the 19th August. Gwernstablau as well as two cottages in the village of Llanwrin were inherited by Jane's sister Mary Roberts (1784-1858). The grave of the Davies Gwernstablau family can still be seen in the churchyard at Llanwrin.

Hugh Davies was baptised in Llanwrin on the 22nd June 1778. It appears that Hugh either succeeded his father as the farmer at Esgair Hir or that Hugh took on the farm himself in early adulthood sometime after 1801. Hugh appeared at Esgair Hir with his sister Mary on the 1841 census. At the time Hugh was employing five live in servants at the farm. Two of these servants included his nephew John Davies and niece Jane Davies - both the children of his sister Elinor. Hugh died at Esgair Hir aged sixty eight of a diseased prostate gland on the 1st August 1846. His death certificate also stated that he had been suffering with kidney problems for several years before his death. He was buried in Llanwrin on the 5th August 1846.

Elinor Davies was born in about 1782. So far I have traced no record of any baptism for her. It is possible that the Esgair Hir Davies family converted to the Methodist religion sometime between 1778 and 1782. Elinor married David Davies (1783-1848), but as of yet I have not found a record of the marriage. David was the eldest son of Hugh Davies of Cilgwyn (who we read about earlier). The couple had at least two children. Jane Davies born in 1819 and John Davies born in 1821. Both children were living at working at Esgair Hir on the 1841 census and are recorded on the 1851 census as having been born in Llanwrin, but again I have found no baptism record for either child. Unlike the other children of John and Mary Davies, Elinor appears to have lived in relative poverty. According to her death certificate Elinor's husband David worked as a woodman. The couple appear on the 1841 census living at Esgair For. David died aged sixty five of influenza at Tybach on the 8th February 1848

17

and was buried in Llanwrin on the 11th February. Elinor appears on the 1851 census living in Tybach with her son and daughter as well as her sister Mary. Elinor died aged seventy five of "old age" at Tybach on the 8th July 1855. At the time of her death she was receiving poor relief from the parish. She was buried in Llanwrin on the 10th July 1855. The fate of her children John and Jane is currently a mystery. On the 1851 census it stated that she had a grandson named John Davies - again he is a mystery at present.

Erglodd Family

The youngest son of John and Mary Davies was Thomas Davies. He was born in around 1789. On the 16th February 1821 he married Mary Morgan (1791-1864) in Llanwrin. The couple remained at Esgair Hir for a number of years after their marriage, as both of their children were born on the farm. However, by 1826 Thomas was farming at Poisnant near Cemmaes. By the 1841 census Thomas was farming at Caedw near Machynlleth. At the time he was employing four live in servants on the farm. By 1851 he was farming at Erglodd in located between Talybont and Taliesin in Cardiganshire. Thomas died aged eighty seven at Erglodd on the 6th March 1876 of "decay of nature."

Thomas was succeeded at Erglodd by his son John Davies. He had been born at Esgair Hir on the 19th November 1821 and was baptised on the farm on the 30th November 1821. John spent his life as a farmer, but was far better known in his lifetime for being a staunch supporter of the Methodist movement. Along with his sister Elizabeth he was one of the founding members of the Methodist Chapel in Talybont and served as a Deacon at the Methodist Chapel in Taliesin. He was also a member of the Calvanistic Methodist Association and one of the leading Calvanistic Methodists in North Cardiganshire. He was well known for his untiring efforts and support of Sunday schools. He also took a keen interest in the national schools in Taliesin and Talybont. Indeed he took great pride in the children of Talybont and Taliesin being well versed and renowned locally for their knowledge of the Bible. During his lifetime he was called the Methodist version of Robert Owen and gained the nickname of "Apostol y Plant" (The Apostle of the children). According to newspaper articles of the time John was a great communicator with children.

In the early 1870s John Davies was also a leading member of the International Order of Good Templars. This society was established to promote temperance or total abstinence from alcohol and was modelled on the Freemasons and had lodges around the country. He was a leading member and public speaker for the society in North Cardiganshire. Newspapers of the time record that John was a humorous and impressive public speaker. He was also well known in the area for his charitable work. He served as a member of the Board of Guardians for Aberystwyth between 1882 and his death in 1887. These boards had been created by the Poor Law Amendment Act of 1834, and were responsible for the running of the local workhouse and payments of relief and care of the poor. "Guardians" were prominent local men and were elected by their fellow ratepayers and would hold meetings every two weeks. They would appoint staff to oversee the day to day running of the workhouses and Overseers of the Poor to collect and distribute the poor rate which was paid by the ratepayers. John died aged sixty five at Erglodd of "general decay brought about by chronic eczema" on the 15th June 1887.

John's sister Elizabeth also lived at Erglodd, likely acting as a housekeeper to her bachelor brother. She also took an interest in local affairs and in helping the needy in the locality. During the 1870s she served as the treasurer of the local Charity Club. This group of local middle class women collected donations from the wealthier people of the district and then distributed the donated money, food, and clothing to the poor and needy of Taliesin every winter. Her brother John would donate a sheep every year to ensure that the poor had a decent meal at Christmas. At some point Elizabeth married a man named William Jones, and the couple had one daughter named Mary Jones. William died soon after the birth of his daughter, and Mary was raised by her mother and her uncle John.

On the 16th October 1876 Mary married James Thomas Morgan (1852-1923) of Maesnewydd near Talybont. James Morgan was a large landowner in the area. He was a well-known farmer in the area as well as being the leading Justice of the Peace in Talybont and a Cardiganshire County Councillor. He also served as a Deacon and the Treasurer of the Methodist Chapel in Talybont. James and Mary had three children. At Maesnewydd Mary and her mother became well known for inviting preachers throughout Wales to dinner parties for religious discussions. Mary died of a stroke at Maesnewydd aged 55 on the 9th April 1906. Elizabeth died at Maesnewydd aged 86 of a "senile heart" on the 29th June 1910. James Morgan died on the 23rd April 1923 with a fortune valued at £5,359 19s 10d.

The Third Thomas Davies Caeadda

Thomas Davies was born on the 26th March 1827 at Caeadda. He was the only known child of Thomas Davies (1788-1875) and Ann Davies (1785-1848). He was baptised at the Sion Calvinistic Methodist Chapel in Llanwrin on the 15th April 1827. According to later newspaper articles he was known in the area as "Tom Davies." Although Thomas was an only child he came from a large family which we have seen were established farmers in the Llanwrin area. On his father's side of the family he would likely have known his cousin Mary Pugh (1808-1885) and her husband John Davies (1805-1886) who farmed at nearby Hendreboeth. His aunt Jane Edwards (nee Davies) (1780-1864) was a regular visitor to Caeadda. On his mother's side his uncle David Davies (1771-1843) farmed at Gwernstablau, while another uncle, Hugh Davies (1778-1846) farmed at Esgair Hir. He would have started working on the farm at a young age, and would have been taught all about farming by his father, in particular about shepherding. This would have been knowledge which would have been passed down from father to son over many generations, and until the late Victorian era the skills and knowledge would have changed very little.

Shepherds were highly skilled men, and in farming it was the most prestigious job. Thomas's knowledge of sheep, their habits and ailments, and his ability to control a flock would have been good. He would have also been an extremely fit man with great physical stamina as a result of the terrain in which he worked. It is possible that as a young man that he would not have used the now common sheep dog. Many farmers of the era used horses to round up the sheep, much like a cowboy does with cows. In the 1700s and 1800s most sheep farming was based on a breeding flock. The farmer made the bulk of his income from selling lambs for slaughter if he had his own grazing land or lambs to other farmers who had lowland pastures. The shepherd's most difficult task was perhaps rounding up his sheep to take them to his farmstead. This would be done, for example, for preparation of tupping, lambing and shearing. As the hills were not fenced or hedged the sheep would be scattered all over them, so it could take the shepherd up to a week to round up all of his flock. During rounding up, the shepherd would remain in the hills sleeping outdoors until the job had been completed. Typically a mattress could be made up using heather and shelter could be found under trees.

The life of a sheep farmer was dominated by a number of regular events that occurred throughout the year. The annual sheep farmer's cycle began with tupping - putting the ram to the ewe. Hill farmers delayed this to later dates than lowland farmers. Some might delay this until December, while the lowland farmers did it in early autumn. Tupping would last for around a period of four weeks. Lambing was (and still is) the most vital part of the year for a sheep farmer. As a result great care and preparation was taken prior to the lambing season which was usually in March or April. Farmers would build temporary folds with whatever materials they could find, and this would allow the farmer to keep a close eye on the lambs to ensure that everything was going well, and also to care for them and feed them. Also prior to lambing the farmer would have grown grass on his meadows and bought in hay from outside sources in order to have feed for the lambs.

The next big event would be shearing, which generally occurred on hill farms in around June or July. Shearing was a skilled job, which in Victorian times would be done with hand sheers. It was also a job that required a deal of strength and stamina. Prior to the actual shearing, the farmer would round up his flock in order to wash the sheep, which was an essential job as unwashed sheep wool was worth a lot less. Shearing on hill farms would be a popular and big event for the farmer's family as a whole. Traditionally the farmer would work with his neighbours to do the shearing in a bid to pool labour to speed up the process. For example, on the Monday the local farmers would work at Caeadda shearing the sheep. On Tuesday the group would move onto Esgair Llewelyn to shear the sheep there and so on. This allowed shearing to become a social event for the sheep farmers of the area. As the wife's and daughters would prepare meals for the men in the evening. These events would have no doubt included singing, shearing contests and other such entertainments. In Wales, shearing traditionally occurred twice a year. A second round of shearing took place in late September when the sheep were sheared close around the neck and forequarters, or the wool would have been lost during the winter months while the sheep wondered around the rough terrain. During this time the farmers would return stray sheep to their neighbours. Usually neighbouring farmers would look after the sheep for their neighbouring farmers if they came across them.

Once the sheep had been sheared the next job was to brand them. The law required that shepherds brand their sheep to denote their ownership of them. Most commonly this was done in one of three ways. The sheep could be branded with a hot branding iron, its ear could be permanently marked by a clip, or it could be marked by paint. Finally another labour intensive task would commonly occur between October and November when the sheep were salved. The most common disease in sheep was scab caused by parasitic ticks and lice. Sheep dipping was not common during the time of

Thomas Davies. Instead a mix of tar and butter was smeared over the sheep. This was a time consuming and smelly job, but was common from the 1500s until the early 1900s.

The big social events for Thomas would have been the local markets and fairs. During the Victorian era Machynlleth was the main market place in Wales for buyers and sellers. In Machynlleth fairs were held every year on the 1st March, the Monday before the third Thursday in April, 16th May, 26th June, 9th July, 18th September, 21st October and 26th November. Many of these would also have been Hiring Fairs. Their purpose was for labourers to find work on farms - a sort of Victorian jobcentre. Thomas would have attended such fairs in Machynlleth and possibly Dolgellau to employ labourers for the coming year - at this time farm labourers were usually employed on a yearly basis. The fairs though were also big social occasions for the farmer's family and gave the farmer's wife a chance to socialise with other farmer's wives and a chance for the children to enjoy games and other attractions. In fact the modern day fun fair originated from these hiring fairs. Another important event for Thomas would have been market days. Before the market the farmer would have to pick out the sheep and lambs that he wished to sell. Next Thomas would have had to drive his sheep from the hills and down the road to Machynlleth. Sheep sales were held in Machynlleth every year on the 5th May, 25th September and 26th October.

Thomas married Gwen Jones on the 22nd June 1859 at Llanwrin village church. The witnesses at the ceremony were John Davies and Elizabeth Davies. The entry into the wedding register shows us that Thomas was literate, which suggests that he received some form of education as a child. It is possible that Thomas received an education at the National School which was opened in Doll Street, Machynlleth, in 1829. According to the 1891 census could speak only Welsh. However, this should be doubted. The fact that Thomas was literate would suggest that he could speak English. Thomas was also a singer, and sang at a concert in Llanwrin in March 1891.

Thomas was fortunate that he lived during the golden age of British agriculture during the 1850s and 1860s. This was an era when prices were high and many farmers gained significant wealth. This wealth allowed larger farmers to have their children educated and to become almost socially equal to the local landowners. Indeed, in both 1861 and 1871 Caeadda could boast of having three live in domestic servants. Thomas had worked under his father until the 1860s, and sometime between 1861 and

1871 his father retired and Thomas took over the running of Caeadda. However, the golden era of British agricultural came to a sudden end after 1875, and agriculture in Britain as a whole slumped into a major depression which lasted until the First World War in 1914. Worst hit were the crop growing arable farms, however, sheep farmers were also hit by a drop in the value of Welsh wool, with the textile industry preferring the cheaper imports of wool from Australia and New Zealand. This further led to a decline in the price of sheep. Weather conditions in this era also did little to help farmers. For example, between February and March 1885 Wales was hit by a great blizzard which caused loss of life to livestock just before the lambing season.

During the Great Agricultural Depression the face of the countryside changed forever. The farmer's income dropped, resulting in mass unemployment for farm labourers. These labourers left the countryside and moved to the cities to work in factories or on the railways. Many farmers decided the best option was to give up their farms, sell their livestock and find alternative work. As a result many farms that had been in the same families for generations either gained new tenants or were swallowed up into neighbouring farms. Some struggled on with their farms, taking out loans to cover losses and hoping that the situation would correct itself. Unfortunately though many farmers ended up going bankrupt.

Obviously some farmers survived, and Thomas was one of these farmers. As previously recorded, during the good times Caeadda employed a number of live in servants. By 1881 there was only one live in maid employed on the farm, and by 1891 there were no live in servants at all. Indeed, in 1891 there was a border living at Caeadda. During these hard times Thomas would have had his children doing the farm work. It is almost certain that his sons John, Thomas, and David were working for him before his death in 1891. His daughter Mary Winifred was also working on the farm. Therefore there were no labour costs, everybody was working for the good of the family. It is perhaps to his credit as a teacher that John, Thomas, and David were all successful farmers.

Forward looking farmers came up with new income streams during these times. This was essential as not being the farm owner Thomas still had to pay his annual rent to the landlord. Thomas appears to have found a good source of income through forestry work. In May 1881 and April 1891 he sold oak timber from Caeadda at auctions in Machynlleth. Vast quantities of wood were sold at these auctions, suggesting that he was involved in substantial forestry work. The quality of the Caeadda oak was renowned, and the sales were advertised in newspapers throughout the Wales and England - again suggesting that he spoke English, as it was Thomas who would have shown the timber to potential purchasers at Caeadda.

Thomas did not own Caeadda, he was a tenant. During the Victorian age nearly all farms in Wales were owned by the great estates of the era. The landowner maintained the farmhouse, farm buildings, field drainage, fencing etc. The tenant farmer in turn provided the money to purchase livestock, farming implements/equipment, paid labourers wages etc. In many cases the system proved to be beneficial to both parties. The farmer benefitted from the landlords long-term investments, while the landlord benefitted from high rent from a productive farm.

Agricultural Shows started to appear in the Machynlleth area in the 1880s and early 1890s. So far I have only found a record of Thomas entered one of these. He entered the Cemmaes Farmer's Club show and came second for his cob under three years of age.

Thomas died aged 64 at Caeadda on the 15th June 1891 of the Russian flu. He was buried on the 19th June 1891 in Llanwrin. An article in the Aberystwyth Observer of the 4th June 1891 reported about a flu epidemic sweeping through Llanwrin, which led to the temporary closure of the school in the village. Thomas died in this flu epidemic (called the Russian flu) that spread around the world between 1889 and 1894. It was estimated that this epidemic killed one million people worldwide.

Gwen Jones

Gwen Jones was born on Thursday the 14th January 1841 in a temperance hotel located at 19 Clayton Square in Liverpool. She was the eldest child of Ellis Jones (1811-1889) and Mary Jones (1818-1857). She was baptised at St. David's Church in Liverpool on Sunday the 31st January 1841. At some point before 1845 the young family had returned to Esgair Llewelyn - the home of Gwen's maternal grandparents. According to family legend, Ellis and his family returned to Wales because the hotel where he worked burned down. I have not yet verified this event.

At the age of eighteen Gwen married Thomas Davies in the village church in Llanwrin on Wednesday the 22nd June 1859. As a farmer's wife, Gwen had a vital role to play at Caeadda. A Victorian farmer's wife would have been expected to run the farmhouse. This would have included all of the cleaning, cooking, and even some farm work. During this era Caeadda would have been the equivalent of a small self-sufficient community. Near to the farmhouse would have been poultry, pigs and cows. Gwen would have had responsibility for looking after these animals which would have all produced food for the family and labourers of the farm. From the cows Caeadda would have had a small dairy, with Gwen likely making butter and cheese. While the poultry would have produced eggs. She would have also had a kitchen garden, where she would have grown fruit and vegetables. Other tasks would have included baking bread and cake making. All of these types of products were regularly seen at the annual agricultural shows, although Caeadda never entered its homemade products into these events. The most time consuming task for the women on the farm would have been the daily routine of making meals for the family and resident farm labourers. However, Gwen's task would have been somewhat easier, as the Davies family were employing two live in female servants until the agricultural depression came in the 1870s. In this instance Gwen would have taken more of a supervisory role, and in later years her daughter Mary Winifred Davies appears to have taken on the role.

After the death of her husband in 1891, Gwen appears to have taken over the running of Caeadda with her eldest son John Davies. Somewhat unique for a woman of the 1890s, she entered her Welsh rams into the Machynlleth Agricultural Show in August 1892 and 1893 and came second in both years. Gwen and John would have been in charge at Caeadda during the historically harsh winter of 1894-1895. In particular February 1895 was a severe month. Between the 7th February and the 19th February the average temperature was -22C, with it reaching -27.2C on the 11th

February. This would likely have hit Caeadda hard financially due to the loss of livestock in the severe conditions. Indeed may farmers in the Llanwrin area never recovered from the effects of the winter. For example, the Tudor family who were farming at Penlan were forced to borrow heavily to buy new livestock, the gamble failed and they went bankrupt in February 1897. After the death of John in October 1897 she ran Caeadda with the help of her son David Davies.

Gwen was listed on the 1915 electoral roll living at Caeadda with her sons David, Hugh and Griffith. By 1926, the year of her death, she was on the electoral roll living at Caeadda with her sons David (and his wife Harriet) and Griffith. According to the censuses of 1891, 1901 and 1911 Gwen could only speak Welsh. Perhaps surprisingly she was also illiterate, and therefore uneducated. I have seen numerous documents where her name is signed with a cross rather than a signature.

Judging by local newspaper accounts Gwen took a keen interest in local events in Llanwrin, and on numerous occasions manned tea tables - for example at the village celebrations for the coronation of King Edward VII in 1902. She once again manned a tea table during the opening ceremony of the Llanwrin Revolt School in June 1908. Socially I have discovered her name in a few newspaper articles as a guest at weddings. In October 1887 she attended the wedding in Llanwrin of Henry Lester Smith and Jennie Owen. Smith lived in Llanbrynmair and was a prominent in the area, being a member of the Machynlleth Board of Guardians and also the land agent for the Williams-Wynn family in the Machynlleth area. Jennie Owen was a daughter of William Owen of Mathafarn (her brother would later father Trevor Owen Davies). Gwen gave them a pair of vases as a wedding present. On Tuesday the 13th October 1903 she attended the wedding of John Roberts a professor of agriculture at Bangor University, and Jennie Gittins of Llanwddyn at the Methodist Chapel in Lake Vyrnwy. As a wedding present Gwen gave them a set of silver carvers in a Morocco leather case.

Gwen died aged 85 of "probably heart failure" at Caeadda on Sunday the 10th October 1926. Her place of burial is currently unknown, but she was not buried in Llanwrin with her husband. Probate was granted to her sons David Davies and Griffith Llewelyn Davies on Friday the 4th March 1927. Gwen's personal estate was valued at £2,630 11s 2d. In her will, Gwen seems to have attached great importance to her copy of the ten volume Gwyddoniadur - a historic publication in the Welsh language published in parts between 1858 and 1879. In her original will she left these books to her grandson Trevor Owen Davies. However, shortly before her death she changed her will and left the books instead to her youngest son Griffith Llewelyn Davies. Unless the original volumes are still in the family it will remain a mystery as to where these books came from.

Gwen was obviously a formidable and dominant woman who was held in high regard by her children. Even today she is still held in high regard by her descendants. It is perhaps a sign of the respect in which she was held that many of her descendants still display pictures of her.

Jones Esgair Llewelyn Family

The Jones family who lived at Esgair Llewelyn appear to have been a well-connected one and had a big impact upon the Davies family. Esgair Llewleyn itself is an old house, dating from the 1400s. The Jones surname is extremely common in the area, and as a result has been extremely difficult to research. Once again the surviving graves of my ancestors have come to the rescue. We can go back to a man named William Jones (1740-1832). He farmed at Cwmgerwyn, which was a farm located not far away from Esgair Llewelyn. The farm is now long abandoned and no longer exists. William was married to Mary (1737-1817). Both were buried in Talyllyn. What is interesting is that the grave states that Mary died at Esgair Llewelyn on the on the 17th May 1817.

John Jones, one of the sons of William and Mary, was baptised at Talyllyn on Friday the 23rd March 1781. He presumably grew up at Cwmgerwyn and was taught his trade by his father. It is worth remembering that John's mother had died at Esgair Llewelyn in May 1817, therefore it seems reasonable to assume that John had started farming here before his marriage in July of that year.

John Jones married Gwen Lewis (1796-1888) on the 11th July 1817 in Dolgellau. Gwen had been baptised in Dolgellau on the 20th February 1796 and was one the daughters of Owen Lewis (1753-1825) who farmed at Fronoleu, Tabor, near Dolgellau. Owen appears to have been a well-connected and wealthy man. He was also an early supporter of the British & Foreign Bible Society - an organisation set up in 1804 to distribute Bibles, notably they also wrote and distributed Bibles in the Welsh language. Gwen inherited £400 when her father died in 1825. Owen's estate at the time of his death was valued at around £1,000. Owen had married Mary David on the 30th October 1786. Mary lived to the old age of ninety one. She died in Waterloo Street, Dolgellau, on the 16th December 1846. Both Owen and Mary were buried in Dolgellau, unfortunately their gravestone has not survived.

John Jones died at Esgair Llewelyn aged 84 on the 27th June 1865, and was buried in Llanwrin on the 1st July 1865. His death certificate recorded that he died of "old age." Gwen appears to have taken over the management of the farm after her husband's death, employing her son in law Ellis Jones to carry out the strenuous farm work. However, by 1881 her Ellis seems to have taken over with Gwen stepping aside and retiring. Gwen died at Esgair Llewelyn aged 92 of apoplexy (a stroke) on the 11th December

1888. She was buried in Llanwrin on the 14th December 1888. It should be noted that neither John nor Gwen left a will.

John and Gwen's only child was a daughter named Mary Jones who was born at Esgair Llewelyn in late 1818. She was baptised in Llanwrin church on the 7th December 1818. Mary appears to have received some form of education as she was literate. According to legend, young Mary ran off to Liverpool where some relatives owned a hotel. While in Liverpool she married a hotel waiter named Ellis Jones on the the 21st September 1840. He was from Dinas Mawddwy. Just over three months later their first child, Gwen Jones, was born. Little is known for certain about Ellis's early life. Ellis was the son of a skinner (somebody who skinned animals for fur etc) named Hugh Jones. Like Mary, Ellis was literate. The evidence would seem to suggest that a pregnant Mary and Ellis ran off to Liverpool together and eloped. Ellis appears to have worked in a hotel located at 19 Clayton Square in Liverpool, and this is where Gwen Jones was born.

At some point between early 1841 and late 1844 Ellis and Mary had returned to Llanwrin and went to live at Esgair Llewelyn with Mary's parents. For around forty years Ellis was employed on the farm, firstly by his father in law and then by his mother in law. By 1881, Ellis had taken over the running of the farm. Mary died aged only thirty eight on the 29th October 1857 and was buried with her Jones ancestors in Talyllyn. So far I have been unable to track down Mary's death certificate. Ellis died aged 78 on the 24th June 1889 at Esgair Llewelyn of apoplexy (a stroke). He was buried on the 26th June in Llanwrin. Neither Ellis nor Mary left any wills. An article appeared in the Cambrian News on the 5th July 1889 reporting upon the inquest into the death of Ellis Jones. Six weeks prior to his death he had suffered a paralytic stroke which had badly affected his speech. He had been discovered in the morning dead in bed by his daughter (who was not named).

The Children of Ellis and Mary Jones

We have already seen about the life of Gwen Jones, the eldest child of Ellis and Mary. However, the couple had a further five children. Briefly they were as follows.

John Jones - Born at Esgair Llewelyn in 1845, he was baptised in Llanwrin on the 30th June 1845. Sometime between 1881 and 1884 John started farming at Hafodymeirch in Tabor near Dolgellau. On the 13th May 1884 he married Jane Owens (1848-1893) at the Ebenezer Chapel in Llanuwchllyn, Merionethshire. She was a member of the Owens family who had farmed for generations in Llanuwchllyn. The couple had one son and three daughters. In 1900 he was appointed the Treasurer of Festri Tir Stent - an area of common grazing land on the slopes of Cadir Idris that was managed by a committee. John died aged 64 of a heart attack at Hafodymeirch on the 15th January 1910. He was buried at Tabor Chapel, near Dolgellau. His personal estate was valued at £162 10s. His wife was not buried with him, but was buried in Llanuwchllyn with her family.

Mary Jones - Born on the 28 March 1847 at Esgair Llewelyn and baptised in Llanwrin on the 13th July. On the 23rd December 1881 she married David Evans (1842-1928) at the New Siloan Chapel in Barmouth. The couple had two sons and two daughters. They farmed at Nantygwrddail, near Arthog. Curiously the family of David Evans had farmed at Hafodymeirch before Mary's brother John Jones. Mary died of stomach cancer aged only thirty nine on the 18th December 1896. She was buried at Tabor Chapel, near Dolgellau. She did not leave a will but administration of her estate was given to her husband and was valued at £108 12s.

Owen Jones - Born at Esgair Llewelyn on the 1st May 1849 and baptised in Llanwrin on the 11th June. Owen served an apprenticeship in carpentry, which he had completed by the time of his death. He died prematurely aged twenty two at Esgair Llewelyn on the 13th October 1871 of consumption (tuberculosis). Owen had suffered from the disease for nine months before his death. He was buried in Llanwrin.

William Jones - William Jones who took over the farm after the death of Ellis Jones in 1889. William had been born at Esgair Llewelyn on the 8th February 1852 and baptised in Llanwrin on the 3rd June. During the 1890s William became a prominent member of the Aberllefenni community, becoming a financial contributor to the Methodist Chapel in the village and socialising with the Jones family of Llwydiarth Hall. In March 1892 the

Llanwrin parish officers, chaired by the Reverend Canon Silvan Evans, appointed William Jones as an Overseer of the Poor for the townships of Glanfechan and Blaen Glesrych. In the days before welfare benefits, an Overseer of the Poor was responsible for the collection and distribution of relief in the parish. He was fully empowered to evict the poor from the parish if he felt they were not genuine or if they were outsiders to the community. In the early 1900s William appears to have retired to Esgair Neiriau (which was also called Esgair Merion) and left the running of Esgair Llewelyn to his nephew William Davies. During the first two decades of the 1900s, the local landowners sold off most of their farms. In most cases the tenants purchased the farms at bargain prices. William appears to have purchased both Esgair Llewelyn and Esgair Neiriau. I have not established when this happened, but it was after June 1908. William Jones died of a stroke at Esgair Neiriau aged seventy three on the 26th May 1925. His personal estate was valued at £2,504 18s 6d. He was buried in Llanwrin, however, he has no gravestone. The death of William Jones marked the end of the Jones family involvement in the local area, and his will saw the division of the Jones family fortune. The Esgair Llewelyn and Esgair Neiriau farms were in theory merged into Caeadda with them being inherited by David Davies and Griffith Llewelyn Davies. Indeed, the brothers formed a business partnership to run the farms in 1932. What happened to the farms after 1932 is currently unknown. However, what is certain is that neither David Davies nor Griffith Llewelyn Davies ever lived at either of the properties.

Elinor Jones - Born at Esgair Llewelyn on the 11th October 1856. She was not baptised in the church at Llanwrin, which might suggest that the family had converted to Methodism sometime between 1852 and 1856. She spent her entire life at Esgair Llewelyn and became the housekeeper at the farm. In March 1882 she was one of the young local women who organised a party for the villagers in Aberllefenni in the Sunday School. She died aged only 39 at Esgair Llewelyn on the 5th January 1896. She had been suffering from an abscessed liver for five months before her death. She was buried in Llanwrin.

The Children of Thomas and Gwen Davies

Thomas and Gwen had twelve children, all of whom survived infancy. All of the children seem to have been educated, in an era when many were illiterate. A National School was opened in Llanwrin in 1876, but before then the children of Llanwrin would have relied on either a Sunday school or a daily walk to school in Machynlleth. However, it should be noted that compulsory education was not introduced in Britain until 1880 for children aged between five and ten, the minimum leaving age was raised to eleven in 1893 and twelve in 1899.

This was an era where the schools taught only in English, and the use of Welsh was actively discouraged. There is little doubt that the children of Thomas and Gwen would have faced this form of discrimination. During this time the Welsh language was considered by the English to be backward, and educated opinion was convinced that the Welsh people were being held back by their language. Some schools in Wales even adopted the practice of only employing English teachers, and some schools used the infamous "Welsh Not" to punish children who used their native language.

Nevertheless, all of the children of Thomas and Gwen seem to have achieved success in life. Indeed, many went on to own their own farms. Perhaps this is all the more remarkable in that they nearly all stayed in the Mid Wales area and achieved success during an era of agricultural depression. This generation of the family might even be called the Golden Generation.

John Davies

John was born on the 17th August 1861 at Caeadda. He was the only child of Thomas and Gwen to be baptised at Llanwrin parish church, his baptism taking place on the 7th October 1861. John would have worked with his father (and likely grandfather) at Caeadda. His father would have raised him to become a farmer and would no doubt have taught John all he knew about shepherding.

John was twenty nine years old when his father died in March 1891. There is little doubt that he succeeded his father as the farmer at Caeadda. It appears that he formed a partnership with his mother in the running of the farm. During the mid-1890s John entered a number of events at local agricultural shows. At the August 1893 Corris Agricultural Show he won first prize for the quality of his Welsh Mountain Ewes, and finished third in the sheepdog trials at the same event. In the same month he won the sheep shearing trials at the Machynlleth Agricultural Show. He also won the Talybont Sheepdog Trials in October 1895 with his sheepdog Fly.

I have found an article in the Cambrian News dated the 13th March 1891 which mentions celebrations that occurred in Llanwrin to celebrate the birth of a son to Sir Watkin and Lady Wynn. At this event John conducted the the Llanwrin Glee Club choir. On the 24th January 1894 he again conducted a Llanwrin choir, this time at a local musical event held at the school.

John died unexpectedly at the young age of thirty six of a heart attack at Caeadda on the 26th October 1897. An obituary above states that John had been complaining of ill health for a month or so before his death. His mother was away from home when he died, his death being registered by his brother Thomas. He was buried in Llanwrin on the 29th October 1897. John never married and left no will. With his next eldest brother Thomas newly installed as the farmer of Penlan and in turn the next eldest Ellis a chemist in London, John's status as the farmer at Caeadda was inherited by David Davies. David would go on to farm at Caeadda for over sixty years.

Thomas Davies

Thomas Davies was born at Caeadda on the 13th February 1864. As a teenager and young adult he almost certainly worked at Caeadda learning his trade off his father and also possibly his grandfather. After his father's death in 1891, he remained at Caeadda working for his brother John. He remained at the farm until early 1897, when he left the family home to go and run his own farm at the age of thirty three. Penlan became available in around March 1897, so it is likely that Thomas became the tenant of that particular farm at that time. Penlan is situated a few miles north of Caeadda and is in the mountains above the hamlet of Ceinws. Penlan was a large farm during the time of Thomas Davies, comprising nearly 900 acres.

In September 1909 the farm was put up for sale by its owner. It is possible that Thomas was the purchaser at a cost of £1,890 - what is certain is that Thomas remained at Penlan after the sale. During the early 1900s the majority of farms in the Llanwrin area were sold by their landlords and it was usually the tenants who purchased the properties at bargain prices. In farming the era was something like the privatisations that occurred in Britain in the 1980s. The reason for the sales were the depressed land values because of the prolonged agricultural depression (1870-1940) and the increasingly high levels of taxation on inherited wealth which financially hit the landowners in the early 1900s. The advertisements for the sale of Penlan provides us a good look at the extent of Thomas's farm. Penlan was 866 acres in size and was mainly a sheep farm, but also contained arable land and valuable woodlands. As well as the farmhouse, Penlan also included a stable, cow houses, wain house and a shed. Up to this point Thomas had been paying an annual rent of £100 for the farm.

Like is younger brother David, Thomas also entered his livestock into local shows. However, Thomas was not as prolific and only entered a small number of contests. At the August 1901 Machynlleth Show he won first prize for his Welsh yearling ram which had been grazed on the mountain from May to August 1901. At the August 1902 Corris Show he came first and second with his Welsh Mountain Wethers.

Thomas appears to have taken a keen interest in local affairs. In April 1896 he was elected onto the Llanwrin Parish Council, and was re-elected in April 1898. Parish Councils had been created by the Local Government Act of 1894. They were made up of between five and fifteen elected members. The first elections had taken place in April 1895, and elections were held annually. In 1901 an act of parliament changed terms of office from one year to three years. Therefore we can assume for the moment that Thomas served on the Llanwrin Parish Council at least between 1896 and 1899. In May 1905 he was appointed as an Overseer of the Poor for the parish of Llanwrin by the Machynlleth Board of Guardians. In April 1916 he was once again appointed as an Overseer of the Poor. In this post Thomas was responsible for collecting poor relief money from the local rate payers and then distributing the money to the needy poor in the parish. At this time there were no welfare benefits, and therefore Thomas has the power to deny payments to anybody who he deemed to be unworthy, and he could also eject outsiders from the parish. Usually this post would be held for a year, and the appointees would be amongst the most prominent men in the parish.

Thomas served as a member of the committee that organised the Corris Agricultural Show in August 1902 and August 1903. In December 1902 he was one of the organisers of a concert from the benefit of the Sion Methodist Chapel in Llanwrin. From around 1902 until 1907 he served as one of the managers of the national school in Llanwrin - he had been appointed by the parish council. On the 1st December 1914 he was one of the organisers of a public meeting in Pantperthog so that the recruiting officer from Machynlleth could address the young men of the locality.

Thomas married Mary Davies (1871-1937) on the 7th February 1911 at the Congregational Chapel in Baker Street, Aberystwyth. The marriage was witnessed by his brother David Davies and Hannah Breese. Mary was one of the daughters of Edward Davies (1833-1904) and his wife Ann Jarman (1838-1907). Edward was a native of Llanfiangel y Creuddyn in Cardiganshire. He had moved to the Llanwrin area after his marriage in the early 1860s. He farmed at Poisnant near Cemmaes. Ann Jarman was from a wealthy farming family from Darowen, Montgomeryshire.

At some point between 1918 and 1924, Thomas moved to and started farming at nearby Gwernstablau. This farm had been sold in June 1917 when the farms of the estate of Sir Watkin Williams Wynn were sold. Along with 89 acres Gwernstablau was purchased by John Reynolds of Carno for £1,650. In April 1918 the tenant of Gwernstablau, a Mrs Margaret Jones, auctioned off her livestock and farming implements. Possibly Thomas moved to Gwernstablau at around this time.

From the mid-1920s onwards it appears that he suffered from ill health. His death certificate states that he had a prostatectomy operation in 1924 to remove part of his prostate gland due to senile enlargement. He wrote his will on the 24th May 1924, so it is very likely that the operation occurred at around the same time. It is also likely that Thomas suffered from the effects of the operation for the rest of his life. Certainly, his days actively farming would have come to an end. Thomas died six years later aged sixty six of bladder cancer and liver failure at the Londonderry Cottage Hospital in Machynlleth on the 22nd March 1930. During this time the diagnosis of cancer would have been like a death sentence and not much could have been done, apart from making his life as painless as possible thereafter.

Probate was granted to David Davies (brother), Trevor Owen Davies (nephew) and David Jarman Davies (brother-in-law) on the 7th May 1930. His personal estate was valued at £4,325 1s 7d. In his will, Thomas left his entire estate to be divided equally between his "devoted wife" Mary and his son Thomas Edward Davies. His wife Mary died on the 13th June 1937. She failed to leave a will but had a personal wealth of £4,390 5s 1d. Administration of her estate was granted to her son Thomas Edward Davies on the 1st October 1937. Both Thomas and Mary are buried in the nonconformist cemetery in Machynlleth. He was buried near to his wife's Davies family and not near any of his own Davies family.

Thomas and Mary had two children. A daughter Mary Davies was born at Penlan on the 10th April 1913, but sadly died only eleven days later on the 21st April of spinal bifida and epilepsy. Their son Thomas Edward Davies was born at Penlan on the 30th March 1916 and he farmed at Gwernstablau until his death on the 20th March 1978.

Anne Davies was born at Caeadda on the 16th February 1866, and was probably named after her paternal grandmother Anne Davies who had died in 1848. She appears to have been known as "Annie." At some point between 1881 and 1891 she left Caeadda and Llanwrin and went to London where she found work as a domestic servant. She worked in the home of Alfred Eckensetin (died 1903) and his wife Margaret (died 1901). At this time it was common for Welsh farmers to send their daughters to work for the wealthy English middle and upper classes. The idea was simple, the girl would learn through experience how to maintain and run a respectable household. The girl would later return to Wales and hopefully marry a farmer and be able to provide a respectable and well run household for her husband. It was the equivalent of a finishing school system for farmer's daughters.

Presumably Annie returned to Caeadda in around 1903 after the death of her employer. She married John Edwards (1867-1946) on the 31st December 1907 at Maengwyn Chapel in Machynlleth. John Edwards was the second son of William Edwards (1839-1910) of Taliesin. William was a stone mason who lived at Temperance House in Taliesin, where he was a prominent member of the local community. In about 1902, John had taken possession of and started farming at Ruel Uchaf in Bow Street, Cardiganshire. John successfully entered events at the Talybont Agricultural Show. During World War I, John was a supporter of the British Red Cross and donated livestock to fundraising events in the area. He also encouraged the use of German prisoners of war as farm labourers during the war due to a shortage of men for manual work during the war.

John Edwards died on the 8th July 1946. Probate was granted to his widow and sons on the 26th August. His personal estate was valued at £1,837 1s 5d. Annie died on the 14th February 1951 aged 84. Probate was granted to her two sons on the 19th March 1951. Her personal estate was valued at £2,384 15s.

The two sons of Annie and John were William Llewelyn Edwards (1908-2000) and Thomas Alfred Edwards (1912-1977). The two brothers ran Ruel Uchaf together. Alfred was well known in the locality as a singer. However, William Llewelyn Edwards achieved note in the area. He was a talented musician, and became well known as an organist, choirmaster, and composer of hymns.

Ellis Jones Davies was born at Caeadda on the 5th April 1868. He was the only son of Thomas and Gwen who did not take up farming. This might appear to be something of a mystery, but we should also consider that Owen Jones Davies and Hugh Davies both served apprenticeships outside of farming before returning to the family trade. At some point between 1881 and 1891 Ellis left Llanwrin to move to London where he sought a career as a chemist. At first it might seem like a strange occupation for a farmer's son to pursue in Victorian Britain. However, Ellis very likely as a child would have worked on Caeadda assisting his father. In the Victorian era the farmer would have usually acted as his own vet, and this would have involved making up treatments for the animals. So it is possible that Ellis was trained by his father in this respect.

In 1891 Ellis was boarding at 2 Milverton Street in Lambeth and was a pharmaceutical student. The house was occupied by Henry Marjaram (a carpenter) and his family. Two other students were lodging at the house - David Jones (aged 23) and John Shearman (aged 21). Curiously David Jones was from Machynlleth, so it would seem likely that Ellis and David had known each other back in Wales. Ellis was apprenticed to a Lambeth based chemist named William Hooper. The basic skills that Ellis would have needed was to be literate and numerate. Good manners and a presentable appearance were also vital as a chemist needed to inspire confidence. Between 1895 and 1898 Ellis completed his apprenticeship and opened up his own chemist store at 120 Seymour Street, Euston Square, London.

Ellis died at Caeadda of rheumatic fever and heart failure on the 16th October 1898 at the age of thirty. He was buried on the 19th October 1898 in Llanwrin. He never married and had no children. Probate was granted to his mother on the 18th November 1898. His personal estate was valued at £124 12s 1d.

David Davies

David Davies was born at Caeadda on the 6th January 1870. David spent his entire life at Caeadda and saw many changes during his lifetime. He certainly started working on the farm at a young age, learning about farming from his father. He was likely amongst the first pupils of the national school in Llanwrin, which was opened in the village in 1876. Unlike some of his siblings, I have found no record of David being musical, he certainly does not appear to have sang at local events. However, he did dress up in the costume of the Bavarian Alps at a lecture given in Llanwrin in March 1890. His father died in 1891 when David was twenty one. He appears to have remained at Caeadda working for his elder brother John.

After the death of John Davies in 1897 it appears that David became a sort of business partner to his mother. Therefore, aged twenty seven, David became the farmer at Caeadda. The partnership with his mother appears to have lasted until her death in 1926. From her will, David inherited her share of the business, and in consequence became the outright owner of the farm. Along with his mother, he appears to have purchased the farm sometime between 1916 and 1922.

As a farmer David proved to be a very capable shepherd and in the early 1900s entered local sheepdog trials. At the September 1908 Machynlleth Sheepdog Trials he came fourth, one place behind his brother William. At the 1909 trials he came second and won an award of £3. At the October 1910 trials he came second out of forty shepherds. He also entered his livestock into local agricultural shows, most notably the annual Machynlleth Agricultural Show where he won countless prizes for the quality of his rams and ewes. He had also entered the Corris Show in 1901 and 1902 and came first for both his Welsh mountain ewes and his Welsh rams. At the Talybont & North Cardiganshire Show in September 1910 he was a judge for sheep shearing. There appears to be little doubt that David Davies was one of the leading and best known farmers of the Machynlleth area during his lifetime.

Farming essentially remained the same as in the days of his father Thomas Davies. However, a number of changes did occur. From the 1920s onwards mechanisation would have slowly crept into the farming world of mid Wales. With the use of machinery such as tractors, the need to employ labourers decreased as certain tasks became quicker and less labour intensive. Likewise, the introduction of electricity allowed farmers to use electrical clippers during sheering. This again changed the nature of the work, as the farmer no longer had to use the old labour intensive and time consuming hand shears.

Perhaps the most controversial change in sheep farming was the introduction of sheep dipping. Sheep scab had been a problem in sheep farming for hundreds of years, and for many years farmers had made up their own salving remedies to prevent the disease occurring. In the 1830s a man named William Cooper had begun selling his sheep dip - a mixture of arsenic and sulphur. The process simply involved the dipping of sheep in a bath of the chemical liquid. In November 1902, David attended a meeting of the farmers of the Machynlleth district held at the Wynnstay Hotel in Machynlleth. The Montgomeryshire Farmers Union had proposed to make it a requirement that members had to dip their sheep twice a year and also had to dip any sheep that they sold and also dip any new sheep that they purchased. Nearly all of the farmers were opposed to the proposals, but the majority declared that they were willing to dip sheep once a year. David Davies spoke at the meeting and was opposed to sheep dipping. He declared that his belief was that sheep scab was both unpreventable and untreatable, therefore in his view dipping was a waste of time and money. In 1907 the government made sheep dipping a legal requirement. To ensure compliance, a policeman was required to be present during dipping to make sure that the entire flock was dipped.

On the 24th April 1923 he married Catherine Harriet Pugh (1880-1972) in Maengwyn Chapel, Machynlleth. The wedding was witnessed by his brother Griffith Llewelyn Davies and Harriet's niece Sarah Gwendolen Jane Jenkins - interestingly the witnesses later married each other. Harriet was one of the daughters of John Pugh (1834-1912) who had farmed at Glyncaerig and Alltddu. Her brother, William Griffith Pugh (1877-1953) was one of the large farmers of the district, having inherited Glyncaerig (near Cemmaes). David and Harriet had no children. Despite this, it is likely that David was a father figure to his nephew Trevor Owen Davies and also to his younger brother Griffith Llewelyn Davies. Indeed, Trevor inherited the bulk of David's estate, while David and Griffith worked together at Caeadda for over twenty years. Griffith's eldest son, David William Davies, also worked at Caeadda under David Davies, but tragically died aged only twenty at the farm in 1951. When his uncle,

William Jones (1852-1925) died, David and his brother Griffith inherited the Esgair Llewelyn and Esgair Meirion farms. David also inherited £500. In 1932 the two brothers drew up a formal business agreement to run the farms. At the moment the fate of the partnership and the family involvement with Esgair Llewelyn is unknown.

David died at Caeadda aged ninety of heart failure on the 7th October 1960. Probate was granted to his nephew Trevor Owen Davies on the 22nd November 1960. His personal estate was valued at £24,814 0s 4d. David's widow carried on living at Caeadda until 1966 when she moved to Pencoed in Cemmaes. She died aged ninety two of a stroke at Bronglais Hospital in Aberystwyth. Both David and his wife are buried in the nonconformist cemetery in Machynlleth.

Mary Winifred Davies was born on the 6th April 1872 at Caeadda. She was named after her maternal grandmother and her mother - Winifred being the English variation of Gwen. She appears to have spent her entire life on the farm, later becoming something of a housekeeper at Caeadda. Her role most likely included making dairy products, looking after the poultry, baking, cleaning and making meals for the household.

Mary never married but had an illegitimate son named Trevor Owen Davies, who we will learn more about later. The father of Trevor was Owen Griffith Owen. A short obituary for him appeared in the Cambrian News dated the 25th November 1898.

"Death of Mr. Owen Mathafarn - The death took place on Friday, after a long illness, of Mr. Owen Griffith Owen, Mathafarn, the last surviving son of the late William Owen Mathafarn. The deceased belonged to an old and well-known family. He had served for some years on the Montgomeryshire County Council and was a member of the Llanwrin Parish Council at the time of his death. He was thirty-five years of age. The funeral, which was a private one, took place on Tuesday, the interment taking place in Corris. The Reverend T.F. Roberts officiated at the house and the Reverend R.J. Edward, Corris, at the graveside."

As well as raising her own son Trevor, she no doubt helped to raise her younger siblings as well. Mary died aged fifty of tuberculosis at Caeadda on the 27th March 1922. She was buried at Llanwrin. It might be interesting to note that she was the last member of the Davies family to be buried at this location. At the time of her death she would have been aware that her son Trevor was applying for a place at Oxford University.

Owen Jones Davies

Owen Jones Davies was born on the 7th September 1875 at Caeadda. He was named after his maternal uncle Owen Jones who had died in 1871. Owen was at Caeadda until at least 1891, and would have no doubt worked on the farm learning about farming from his father. At some point in the 1890s he completed a five year apprenticeship in London, working in a department store in Kentish town. The store was called C & A Daniels and was one of the large prosperous London stores. Owen was apprenticed in the dry goods department (something like a modern day men's clothing store). However, by late 1897 he was back in Llanwrin and was employed as a farm worker by his brother Thomas at Penlan. Some his apprenticeship might have covered the period between 1892 and 1897.

Between 1897 and 1902 he was employed by his elder brother Thomas Davies at Penlan, Ceinws. He is mentioned in numerous local newspapers in early 1898. Between January and March 1898 a number of benefit concerts were held in Ceinws to raise money. Owen won the tenor contests at these events. In one he sang "Maer lan gerllan." Indeed, he was noted in the area for being a talented tenor. In about 1902 he left Wales and immigrated initially to the United States. Despite great effort no record of Owen entering the United States has been found at the moment, but he most likely travelled by ship from Liverpool. Why he left Wales is another mystery, one explanation is that he wished to go and visit a friend in America. Perhaps he believed that he could make something of himself in America.

Initially he settled in Denver, Colorado, where he worked for a year as a timekeeper in a gold and silver mine. In this job he would have simply recorded the times that individual workers started and finished work. Having saved some money from this job, he next moved to Almira in the state of Washington, where he formed a business partnership with three fellow Welsh immigrants and purchased a farm. At this time Almira had a community of Welsh immigrants. In 1905 they sold the farm to a railroad company and made a large sum of money from the sale.

After this sale, Owen and a number of fellow Welsh immigrants relocated to Wood River in Alberta, Canada. The Wood River area was settled by Welsh immigrants between 1900 and 1910 when the population reached a peak of two hundred. The main town of the area, Ponoka, was founded in

1905. Here Owen formed another partnership and bought untouched land and became a farmer. The two men built on the land and bought five hundred sheep to help to clear the land, and the hired Native American Indians to help with the work. To help raise money during this time, Owen transported cream to the Earlville Creamery from the farms in the area. In 1909, Owen nearly met with disaster when a bad grass fire in the region burned down his barns and granaries. Fortunately for Owen, a neighbour allowed him to use his barns while Owen rebuilt his. In the decades that followed Owen slowly extended his farm by buying out various neighbours. In time he also bought out his business partner and took full control of the farm. Ultimately he built up a farm of roughly 600 acres.

Socially, Owen became one of the leading members of the area and helped to establish a Welsh community in the area. In Wood River Owen became closely associated with the local Zion Welsh Presbyterian Church and the Wood River Festival (a sort of Eisteddfod). The church held regular Welsh language services until around 1929. By this time many of the original Welsh settlers had either died or moved on and the upcoming generation and new residents were English speakers, thus the language had died out in the area within a few decades. For decades he was in charge of the church ladies choir - his greatest successes being that he directed the Wood River Festival award winning choirs of the 1930s.

After leaving Wales he dropped his middle names of Jones became known as Owen G. Davies. The G stood for Gwrin – after St Gwrin to whom Llanwrin church is dedicated to. On the 24th December 1913 he married fellow Welsh immigrant Mary George (1886-1917). William George, his wife and nine children, had arrived in Ponoka in 1912 and came from the town of Cilgerran in Pembrokeshire Where William had been a farmer. Mary was the eldest child. She died in 1917 aged only thirty. When his wife died, Owen employed Mrs Clara Cook (1876-1960) as his housekeeper. Clara was an English woman from Lincoln who had immigrated with her husband to Alaska in 1901, and arrived in Ponoka in 1912 where she found work in the Ponoka Mental Hospital. Mrs Cook worked for Owen for many years and became a mother figure to Owen's surviving son Iorwerth Davies (1916-2007). She also became a dedicated member of the Zion Church with Owen. In 1943, Owen and Mrs Cook took in a twelve year old orphan called Harry Thacker, they cared for him until he was sixteen. Mrs Cook died aged eighty three in 1960. Owen died aged eighty three on the 8th December 1958 and was buried at his beloved Zion Welsh Presbyterian Church in Ponoka.

William Davies

William Davies was born on the 11th January 1878 at Caeadda and was undoubtedly named after his maternal uncle William Jones. In January 1889, he won an award at a local Eisteddfod for his story about a boy learning to sing. William was living at Caeadda at least up until early 1903. In April 1903 he represented the Davies Caeadda family at the funeral of Daniel Silvan Evans (1818-1903). Evans was a famed promoter of the Welsh language, his most notable achievement was writing and publishing the first Welsh to English dictionary letter by letter between 1887 and his death in 1903. Unfortunately he never finished the dictionary. At his funeral, William was part of the procession that walked from Llanwrin to the burial ground in Cemmaes. Also at the funeral was William Jones of Esgair Llewelyn.

He was only thirteen when his father died in 1891, therefore William most likely learned the farming trade from his elder brothers John, Thomas and David. When his elder brother Thomas moved to Penlan in 1897, nineteen year old William appears to have remained at Caeadda, working firstly under his brother John and then David. Like David, William was a talented shepherd, and entered a number of local sheepdog trials during the first decade of the 1900s. At the October 1899 Staylittle Sheepdog Trials he finished second, he again came second at the October 1902 trials. At the October 1900 Staylittle Sheepdogs Trials William tied with Tom Jones of Aberhosan. To decide who would win the trophy a rerun occurred which William unfortunately lost. He came second in the August 1902 Abergynolwyn Show. At the October 1907 Machynlleth Sheepdog Trials he came forth and won 7s 6d. In the October 1908 trials he finished third, one place ahead of David Davies. At the September 1909 trials he finished third (David Davies finished second). In the September 1909 Llanbrynmair Sheepdog Trials he came second and in October 1910 he entered the same trials but this time failed to finish within the top five.

William married Jane Evans (1880-1947) at the registry office in Machynlleth on the 22nd June 1901. The marriage was witnessed by William's sister Mary Winifred Davies and David Morgan. In 1901 Jane was living with Edwin and Elizabeth Hamer (her sister and brother in law) at a Llanwrin farm called Cae Cyno. The couple were married in a registry office due to the fact that Jane was pregnant at the time of the marriage. She was one of the daughters of John Evans, who farmed at Faedre Fawr, which is near the hamlet of Llawryglyn in the mountains surrounding Trefeglwys. The nearest town of note being Llanidloes which was about five miles away. Unfortunately the child was born prematurely at Cae Cyno on the 18th August 1901 and died. Sadly the daughter was never given a name. In all, the couple would have seven children.

Sometime between April 1903 and October 1904 the couple moved to and started farming at Esgair Llewelyn. William seems to have taken over the running of the farm from his uncle William Jones, who retired to Esgair Neirion. Why William Davies left Esgair Llewelyn is currently unknown, but he must have had a good reason to leave a farm that had been in the family at that time for nearly one hundred years. However, a report from the Sanitary Inspector to the Llanwrin Parish Council might give us the reason as to why Esgair Llewelyn was abandoned. In April 1906 the council had reported upon the poor sanitary conditions of the house, the issue was raised again in May 1907 and June 1908. It appears that modifications/repairs never took place. William and his family vacated the farm sometime between 1911 and 1913. I have so far found no evidence that anybody has lived at Esgair Llewelyn since this time.

On the March 1911 census, Cae Cyno was described as being a nine room farmhouse and was still being farmed by Edwin Hamer and his wife. Cae Cyno was put up for sale by its owner in September 1911, so it seems possible that William rented it off the purchaser from this time. It might also be worth noting that Edwin Hamer took over the Evans family farm of Faedre Fawr. So it is possible that Edwin moved back to Llawryglyn when John Evans died and that William succeeded Edwin at Cae Cyno at the same time. This question needs more researching as of yet I have not found the date that John Evans died.

It was at Cae Cyno that William died aged only forty of the Spanish Flu on the 28th November 1918. The Spanish flu lasted from January 1918 until December 1920 and ultimately killed between fifty and one hundred million people worldwide. William was buried with the Davies family in Llanwrin. William failed to leave a will, but administration of his estate was granted to his widow Jane on the 7th March 1919. His estate was valued at £1,832 10s 9d.

In March 1919 his widow sold all of his livestock, farming implements etc at an auction at Cae Cyno. After William's death Jane moved back to her childhood home of Faedre Fawr, taking her children with her. Jane's sister, Elizabeth Hamer, died in 1924. In 1925, Jane married her widowed brother-in-law Edwin Hamer (1860-1946). Together the couple farmed at Faedre Fawr, at one point being assisted by William's son Ellis Jones Davies (1902-1938).

Of note is that a granddaughter of William Davies is the distinguished harpist Elinor Bennett, whose husband Dafydd Wigley was at one time the leader of the political party Plaid Cymru.

Hugh Davies was born on the 26th August 1880 at Caeadda. He was living on the farm until at least 1891. In 1901 he was working as a draper's assistant in Overton, Flintshire. He was working for Lewis Evans, who was a native of Dolgellau. However, he was back at Caeadda by 1904 working on the farm alongside his elder brother David. By this time his elder brothers John and Ellis were dead, Thomas was farming at Penlan, Owen had gone to Canada, and William was farming at Esgair Llewelyn. Therefore perhaps Hugh was an obvious choice to work at Caeadda under David.

As well as working on the farm, Hugh involved himself with the school in Llanwrin. In June 1904 a tea party was held for the families who sent their children to the school. Hugh was given a special mention of thanks for his work as a choirmaster to the children. Between 1907 and 1908 he was a member of a local Llanwrin committee which was tasked with establishing a revolt school in Llanwrin to replace the unpopular national school.

In September 1907 he was fined 10 shillings for riding his horse and cart without reins. He appears on the 1915 electoral roll as living at Caeadda. In April 1915 Cwmrhwyddfor in Talyllyn became available. It might have been around this time that Hugh initially rented or purchased the farm. It appears that he borrowed money off his mother for this purpose, and the loan was written off in her will. What is certain is that Hugh moved to Cwmrhwyddfor sometime between 1915 and 1922.

Hugh never married and had no children. However, Hugh seems to have taken a shine to the sons of his younger sister Jane - Evan Nutting and Thomas Davies Nutting. The Nutting family lived at nearby Rhiwogof. Indeed, Thomas Davies Nutting worked for Hugh at Cwmrhwyddfor. At some point Hugh retired from the farm and went to live with his widowed sister Ellen at Bodowen in Aberdovey.

Hugh died at Bronglais Hospital, Aberystwyth, on the 30th May 1966. Probate was granted to his nephew Thomas Davies Nutting on the 14th September 1966. Hugh's personal estate was valued at £8,555. In his will he left Cwmrhwyddor to his nephew Thomas Davies Nutting and left his shares in Merion Creameries Limited to his nephew Evan Nutting of Rhiwogof. Hugh had obviously loved his life at Cwmrhwyddor, and in his will he requested that his body be cremated and the ashes scattered at the farm. Cwmrhwyddor is still in the family today.

Ellen Louisa Davies was born at Caeadda on the 1st January 1883. On the 24th January 1894, she won an award for Bible reading in the under 16 category at an Eisteddfod held in Llanwrin. In 1901 she was living with her brothers Thomas and Owen at Penlan. It is very likely that Ellen was working for her then unmarried brother as some sort of housekeeper.

On the 3rd April 1901 she married Robert Hughes (1864-1941) at the Bethel Chapel in Towyn. The marriage was witnessed by Hugh Hughes (Robert's brother) and Mary Winifred Davies (Ellen's sister). The couple had no children. Robert was one of the sons of Hugh Hughes (1821-1892) who had farmed at Tyddyndu, near Dolgellau. Upon his father's death in 1892, Robert inherited £1,000.

After their marriage in 1901, the couple appear to have lived and farmed at Rhiwogof, Talyllyn. Robert had been farming here since at least 1900 - the year in which his Welsh mountain rams won first prize at the Corris Agricultural Show. In the Corris Agricultural Shows of 1901 and 1902 he competed against his brother-in-law David Davies Caeadda with his Welsh mountain rams, but on both occasions finished second to David. In 1909, Robert was fined 10 shillings in the Dolgellau magistrate's court for his failure to report six of his sheep that were affected with scab. By 1910, the couple had moved to Dolffanog Fach.

An apology by Maggie Hughes to Ellen appeared in the Cambrian News in February 1918 and seems to involve some unknown rumours spread by Ellen's neighbour, who also happened to be Robert Hughes's niece. Robert took an interest in the local affairs of Corris. In March 1907, he was elected to the Corris Parish Council as a Liberal. He was re-elected in April 1910. Therefore we know for certain that he served as a Corris Parish Councillor between 1907 and 1913. In September 1917 he attended a public meeting at the Corris Institute, where he was appointed to a committee who were given the responsibility or erecting a memorial in memory of the local men who had died in World War I.

By 1925, Ellen and Robert had retired to Aberdovey, where they lived at a house called Bodowen. Robert died here on the 24th November 1941 and probate was granted to Ellen on the 2nd March 1942. His personal estate was valued at £1,671 12s 4d. In his will Robert left all of his estate to his widow on the condition that she provided in her own will for the children of William Rowlands Nutting and Jane Davies. Robert and Ellen were childless and appear to have taken a keen interest in the Nutting children. During the 1960s Ellen's brother Hugh retired and came to live with her. By the late 1960s Ellen was living at the Bryntegwel Nursing Home in Aberdovey. She died here at the age of eighty five of a stroke on the 5th June 1968.

Jane Davies was born on the 10th August 1884 at Caeadda. On the 2nd April 1909 the pregnant Jane Davies married William Rowlands Nutting (1885-1966) in the registry office in Machynlleth. The wedding was witnessed by Thomas Davies and Catherine Nutting. William was the son of Evan Nutting of Llanllugan near Llanfair Caereinion. Here Evan lived and farmed at Vrongreen. Closer to Llanwrin William was the grandson of William Rowlands who farmed at Dolwen. William Rowlands had served on the Llanwrin Parish Council with Jane's brother Thomas Davies Penlan in the 1890s. William Rowlands died in 1914 leaving an estate valued at £838. His father, Evan Nutting, died in 1924 leaving an estate valued at £2,247.

On the 1911 census Jane was living with her elder brother Thomas at Penlan, along with her infant daughter Gwen Jones Nutting. She was employed by Thomas as a dairymaid. Her husband was working on his grandfather's farm Dolwen. Between 1912 and 1915, William and Jane finally found somewhere to settle with their growing family. They started farming at Rhiwogof in Talyllyn. It might be worth noting that William's grandfather died in 1914, so possible William inherited enough money to set himself up in farming. This farm had previously been occupied by Jane's brother in law Robert Hughes who had left Rhiwogof to farm at Dolffanog Fach. On the 1911 census, Rhiwogof was described as being an eleven roomed farmhouse. At the time the farm was occupied by Humphrey Jones and his family.

According to the will of David Davies, which was written in 1956, Jane and her husband were living at Dolffanog Fach, Talyllyn. In later life, William Rowlands Nutting became a prominent member of the community in Talyllyn, becoming an elder of the Methodist Chapel. William died aged eighty on the 21st April 1966. Jane died aged eighty four at Dolfannog Fach on the 27th May 1969.

Of her children, her eldest son Evan Nutting (1912-2006) was the last of the Davies Caeadda era to be born at Caeadda. In around 1938 he formed a partnership with his brother in law Goronwy Pughe (husband of Gwen Jones Nutting) called Nutting & Pughe to run Rhiwogof. The farm is still in the family today. The descendants of Goronwy Pughe and Gwen Jones Nutting now farm at Caeadda. Jane's youngest son, Tom Nutting, as previously mentioned inherited Cwmrhwyddor from his uncle Hugh Davies. This farm is also still in the family.

Griffith Llewelyn Davies

Griffith Llewelyn Davies was born at Caeadda on the 17th November 1888. In May 1903, he finished sixth out of thirty one competitors in the under 16 category at the Machynlleth and District Sunday School Festival. In June 1904 he was awarded his county exam certificate. For the first forty years of his life he lived and worked at Caeadda. Without doubt his elder brother David would have been a father figure for younger Griffith - David being eighteen years older. It would have been David who would have taught Griffith all about farming and shepherding. Griffith was also likely his mother's favourite child as he inherited the majority of her personal wealth when she died in 1926. He remained at Caeadda until his marriage in 1929.

When his uncle, William Jones (1852-1925) died, Griffith and his brother David inherited the Esgair Llewelyn and Esgair Neiriau farms. In 1932, the two brothers drew up a formal business partnership to run the two farms. Whereas David remained at Caeadda for his entire life, Griffith never went to live at either Esgair Llewelyn or Esgair Neiriau. By the time that the brother inherited the farms, Esgair Llewelyn was likely uninhabitable. The poor state of the property had been commented upon in 1908, so we can imagine it would have been in a poor state with twenty more years of neglect.

He married Sarah "Sally" Gwendolen Jane Jenkins (1903-1992) on the 21st May 1929 in Maengwyn Chapel, Machynlleth. The marriage was witnessed by Trevor Owen Davies (Griffith's nephew) and Gwendoline May Griffiths (Sally's cousin). Sally was a daughter of Thomas Jenkins (1859-1913) who had farmed at Maescelyn, Glasbwll. Thomas had been a leading farmer in the Glasbwll area and had been an elder of the chapel in Glasbwll. He had also been a talented artist and had entered local Eisteddfod with his work. Sally's mother was Elizabeth Ann Catherine Pugh (1871-1906) - a sister of the wife of Griffith's brother David Davies. Orphaned at a young age, Sally was brought up by her uncle William Griffith Pugh (1877-1953) who farmed at Glyncaerig near Cemmaes. William was one of the wealthiest farmers in the area.

After his marriage, Griffith and his new wife went to farm at Tymawr, Ceinws. The couple would have six children. During the Second World War Griffith had Land Girls working on his farm. Griffith died of pneumonia at the Machynlleth Corris & District Hospital on the 16th January 1943 aged fifty four. He was buried in the Nonconformist Cemetery in Machynlleth in an unmarked grave. Griffith failed to leave a will, but administration of his estate was granted to his widow in Bangor on the 31st January 1944. His personal estate was valued at £1,006 6s 4d. Sally moved out of Tymawr shortly after and moved to the nearby village of Corris.

Griffith's eldest son, David William Davies (1931-1951), went to work at Caeadda and sadly died there aged only twenty on the 17th July 1951 of meningitis.

The End of an Era – Trevor Owen Davies

Trevor Owen Davies was born at Caeadda on the 20th November 1895. He was the illegitimate son of Mary Winifred Davies and Owen Griffith Owen (1863-1898). His father lived at Mathafarn in Llanwrin, and was a cousin of Margaret Owen (1866-1941), who married David Lloyd George (1863-1945) - Britain's only Welsh Prime Minister. When Owen died in 1898 his personal estate was valued at £1,858 5s 7d. Trevor does not appear to have benefitted from his father's wealth. Indeed, Owen Griffith Owen failed to leave a will. Trevor spent his childhood at Caeadda. His father figure was his uncle David Davies. This is perhaps confirmed by Trevor referring to David as his father on his army medical forms. It is likely that Trevor would have been raised alongside his uncle Griffith Llewelyn Davies. Both boys would no doubt have been taught about farming by David Davies. According to his military files Trevor was working as a farm labourer for David Davies in 1917. It appears to be fairly certain that Trevor never again took up farm work after serving in the army in World War I.

From a young age Trevor proved to be very able academically, and showed a great interest in religion. Llanwrin fell under the Upper Montgomeryshire District of the Calvinistic Methodists. In April 1909 he scored 91 out of 100 on Matthew 26-28 in the Upper Montgomeryshire Calvinistic Methodist Sunday School Examinations. In June 1914, aged only eighteen, Trevor was put forward for training to become a Calvinistic Methodist Preacher. He took his Preacher's exam in September 1915 and qualified with a score of 200 out of 300. In October 1915, he was granted permission to start preaching by the Upper Montgomeryshire meeting. During this time Trevor gained the nickname of "The Young Preacher."

Between 1913 and 1917 he attended the Machynlleth County School, which had been opened in 1894. The headmaster of the school was Hugh Harries Meyler, a man with an Oxford degree who was noted for being an exceptionally gifted teacher. Meyler was impressed with Trevor's "character, high aims, and serious application to his studies." In July 1917, he received his Higher Certificate of Education from the Machynlleth County School. Previously he had gained a Senior Certificate of Education. He also received a special mark of distinction for his scripture knowledge. Meyler was also greatly impressed by Trevor's talent as a singer, noting "he is a singer of unusual merit and distinction in a land where the standard of music is a high one." In the local newspapers of the time we find a number of mentions of Trevor getting involved with singing activities in the local area. In March 1914, he sang at a fundraising event at the Machynlleth County School for the local Baptist Chapel. In April 1914, he performed in the opera "Aladd-in and Out" that the county school held to celebrate Easter. Trevor played the part of "Phatman" the Prime Minister.

On the 25th January 1916 Trevor travelled to Welshpool, when he enlisted with the British Army under the Derby Scheme. This meant that even though he had enlisted, he would not be called up to serve unless necessary. On the 4th June 1917, Trevor was finally called up to serve his country. However, Trevor never really got to experience a full military life due to chronic ill health. On the 5th January 1918 a medical report was written recommending that Trevor be discharged. The report stated: "Had a severe attack of acute rheumatism in January 1917 which kept him in bed for about fourteen weeks and left his heart affected. Was exempted for about five months owing to his heart condition and was eventually called up on 2 June. Reported sick several times. Was admitted to hospital here (Prees Heath) on 8 September 1917." The report described Trevor's current health as follows: "He still suffers from palpitations and tachycardia (pulse rate 140 per minute) after seventeen weeks stay in hospital, eleven weeks in bed, and bromides. At times there is a systolic murmur present. He has improved of late but would understandably break down in training."

For his trouble, Trevor was awarded three medals. The British War Medal, the Victory Medal and the Silver War Badge. Trevor also made claims against the British Army for compensation, arguing that his military service had negatively affected his health. From his discharge he was granted a pension of 20 shillings per week which lasted up until the 21 August 1918. On the 11th January 1919 he was awarded a pension of 5/6 per week for a period of twenty six weeks (6 months) and a one off gratuity payment of £10. Trevor applied to have the pension extended, but the army formally rejected this application on the 19th September 1919. It was noted that his symptoms had vanished within six months of his discharge.

Between October 1918 and July 1921 he was a student at the University College of Wales in Aberystwyth. Trevor had received the Owen Jones Scholarship to go to Aberystwyth. This scholarship was worth £22 per year and was awarded by the Methodist Theological College in Bala. At Aberystwyth he was very active in the social life of the university, being elected to the Student Representative Council and also being elected as the College Song Singer for all college functions. He was also a member of the university hockey team. In August 1919 he passed his first year exams in Latin, Greek and Philosophy. He graduated from Aberystwyth with a degree in the classics (the study of ancient Greece and Rome). While studying at Aberystwyth, he lived at Brynglas on Brynymor Terrace in Aberystwyth.

From Aberystwyth Trevor went to Oxford University. Here he met with controversy. He applied to two colleges - the traditional Welsh Jesus College and the prestigious Christ Church College. He was accepted by both colleges and chose the more prestigious Christ Church. Unfortunately he neglected to inform Jesus College of his decision, leading to the dean of Jesus College writing a strongly worded letter to the dean of Christ Church describing Trevor as "shabby and discourteous." He gained a second class honours degree in Theology in 1924. After earning his degree he decided to stay on at Oxford to gain a second degree. In June 1925 he was awarded a B.Litt (Bachelor of Letters) degree for his thesis "An Examination of the Augustinian Doctrine of grace and Predestination." He studied for his B.Litt under the supervision of Leonard Hodgson - the theology tutor and dean of divinity of Magdalen College.

Trevor's life after Oxford was recorded in the book *Trevecka (1706-1964)* which was written by his son Gareth Davies in 1971.

The last Principal of the College was the Reverend Trevor Owen Davies B.Litt., M.A. (Oxon), B.A. (Wales), a native of Montgomeryshire, educated at Aberystwyth University and Christ Church, Oxford. He, like many others, chose to remain at Trevecka where he believed his mission lay. He did not confine his activities to his work there. His services as a preacher in Welsh and English were sought throughout Wales. He was for many years a member of the Breconshire Education Committee and also served on the BBC Religious Advisory Council. In 1950, he was made a Justice of the Peace for the county of Brecknock.

Trevor had been ordained as a minister in the Presbyterian Church in 1925 soon after leaving Oxford. According to a biographical sketch of Trevor on the Library of Wales website, between 1925 and 1926 he served as a minister in Cilfynydd, Glamorganshire. However, in a letter written in 1926 Trevor himself claimed to have been teaching in a secondary school during this time. Nevertheless, in 1926 Trevor became a professor at

Trevecka College, which is a few miles outside of the town of Brecon. The college was a sort of prep school for future ministers/preachers.

Trevor became a very successful and a senior figure within the Methodist Presbyterian Church, particularly with regard to education. He became the Chairman of the United Colleges Board of his Connexion and was elected Moderator of the Association in the East in 1964. For many years he gave numerous lectures at the universities in Cardiff, Aberystwyth, and Birmingham. The crowning achievement of Trevor's career was when he served as the last principle of Trevecka between 1955 and 1964. He retired in 1964 when the college closed. At some point he built himself a home on the college grounds.

He had married Olwen Jane Phillips (1909-1999) on the 10th August 1933 in Maescar, Brecon. The couple had one son. Olwen was one of the daughters of the Reverend Benjamin Phillips of Merthyr Cynog.

When his uncle David Davies died in 1960, Trevor inherited the bulk of his wealth and Caeadda. Trevor died on the 10th April 1966 of prostate cancer. He was buried in the Siloa Cemetery in Merthyr Cynog. His personal estate was valued at £21,887. After his death Caeadda passed on through the family to the descendants of Trevor's aunt Jane Nutting.

www.ingramcontent.com/pod-product-compliance
Lightning Source LLC
Chambersburg PA
CBHW070403290526
45790CB00004B/1610